20TH CENTURY *music*

1900-20

NEW HORIZONS

Please visit our web site at: www.garethstevens.com
For a free color catalog describing Gareth Stevens Publishing's
list of high-quality books and multimedia programs, call
1-800-542-2595 or fax your request to (414) 332-3567.

Library of Congress Cataloging-in-Publication Data

Hayes, Malcolm.
    1900-20: new horizons / by Malcolm Hayes.
        p. cm. — (20th century music)
    Includes bibliographical references and index.
    Summary: Discusses the influence of people and events worldwide in the first
decades of the twentieth century which led to experiments with dissonance, modern
ballet, and the birth of jazz.
    ISBN 0-8368-3031-8 (lib. bdg.)
    1. Music—20th century—History and criticism—Juvenile literature. [1. Music—20th
century—History and criticism.] I. Title. II. 20th century music.
ML3928.H34   2002
780'.9'04—dc21   2001054221

This North American edition first published in 2002 by
Gareth Stevens Publishing
A World Almanac Education Group Company
330 West Olive Street, Suite 100
Milwaukee, WI 53212 USA

Original edition © 2001 by David West Children's Books. First published in Great Britain
in 2001 by Heinemann Library, Halley Court, Jordan Hill, Oxford OX2 8EJ, a division of Reed
Educational and Professional Publishing Limited. This U.S. edition © 2002 by Gareth Stevens, Inc.
Additional end matter © 2002 by Gareth Stevens, Inc.

Designer: Rob Shone
Editor: James Pickering
Picture Research: Carrie Haines

Gareth Stevens Editor: Patricia Lantier

Photo Credits:
Abbreviations: (t) top, (m) middle, (b) bottom, (l) left, (r) right

AKG London: pages 7(mr), 10(bl, tr), 11(br), 15(tl), 28(mr).
The Art Archive: pages 8(br), 9(br), 12(bl), 13(tr), 19(tr, bl), 25(ml, br).
Mary Evans Picture Library: pages 4(bl), 4-5(t, m), 6(tr), 7(tr, br), 13(br), 16(bl, br), 23(br), 28(bl).
Hulton Getty: cover (br), pages 5(br), 8-9(t), 12-13(b), 14(bl, br), 16(tr), 17(br), 19(br), 20(bl, tr),
    20-21(b), 21(br), 24(tr), 27(tl), 29(tl).
Robert Harding Picture Library: page 29(b).
Lebrecht Collection: cover (m), pages 3, 6-7(b), 8(bl), 9(mr), 10(br), 11(tr), 12(tr), 15(m, br),
    17(tr), 18(bl, tr), 20-21(t), 22(bl, mr), 23(tl), 24(br), 25(tl), 26(tr, br), 27(br), 29(mr).
The Planets ã Consignia plc 1985 (all rights reserved)/Lebrecht Collection: page 27(mr).

Printed in the United States of America

1 2 3 4 5 6 7 8 9 06 05 04 03 02

20TH CENTURY music

1900-20

NEW HORIZONS

Malcolm Hayes

Gareth Stevens Publishing
A WORLD ALMANAC EDUCATION GROUP COMPANY

CONTENTS

In February 1917, a people's revolution dethroned the tsar of Russia and ended the country's imperial monarchy government. Later that year, Vladimir Lenin (on steps, with cap and beard) *and his Communist Bolshevik Party seized power.*

OLD WORLDS AND NEW

OIn 1900, music was poised on the verge of a new age. Over the next twenty years, revolutionary ideas about what classical music could sound like would take hold.

Vienna is where music began to sound distinctly "modern," as composer Arnold Schoenberg and his followers began to explore wild extremes of intensity and dissonance. Paris was the other exciting musical center, where a sequence of ballet scores by a young Russian named Igor Stravinsky announced another explosive musical revolution.

When World War I began in 1914, the stability of European life and culture was swept away for good, but radical ideas about music remained.

Across the Atlantic, the rise of jazz, blues, and ragtime was setting a new course for the future of music. The New World was offering an exciting vision of what music could accomplish.

The Graphophone
Makes Home Happy.
GRAND PRIX, PARIS 1900.

The World's
Best Talking Machine.
You can afford one because prices range from **25/= to £32.**
We can suit you because we have **Thirty-five Different Styles.**
Every One is a Good One.
You are missing one of the greatest pleasures of modern life if you haven't one in your home.
Write for Price Book 17 to—
Columbia Phonograph Co., Gen'l.
122, Oxford Street L..... W.

In the early 1900s, the "Graphophone" and other hand-cranked gramophones were exciting, high-tech instruments that began a new age of home listening.

Music brought encouragement and comfort to soldiers involved in the muddy horrors of trench warfare in World War I.

Igor Stravinsky (1882–1971) grew up in the imperial Russian city of St. Petersburg. His world changed drastically with the Bolshevik Revolution.

CLASSICAL CONTROVERSY

Two great figures towered over the musical world of the Austro-Hungarian and German empires at the dawn of the 20th century. Gustav Mahler (1860–1911) and Richard Strauss (1864–1949) were not only major composers but also two of the finest conductors of their time.

Mahler was famous as both a composer and a conductor. He was an idealist with extremely high musical standards, and he wasn't afraid to make enemies.

RADICAL SYMPHONIST

Although very popular today, Gustav Mahler's music was quite controversial in his lifetime. "A symphony should be like the world," he once said. So his symphonies enormously expanded the 19th-century idea of an orchestral work in four movements. Several of his works use solo and choral voices. His Eighth Symphony, for example, the so-called *Symphony of a Thousand*, requires a huge number of performers. Mahler also drew on the sounds of the wider world around him — birdcalls, military fanfares, and Austrian country dances.

MODERNISM VERSUS TRADITIONALISM

Richard Strauss, who was not related to either of two earlier composers, both named Johann Strauss, began his career as a bold modernist. By the age of twenty-four, he had achieved huge success with the symphonic poem *Don Juan* and was already world-famous when his one-act operas *Salome* and *Elektra* shocked audiences with their gruesome plots and dissonant music. Later in his career, however, Strauss changed the direction of his music, preferring the considerably more traditional, harmonic style of his full-length operas *Der Rosenkavalier* and *Ariadne auf Naxos*.

Hans Pfitzner stands behind the conductor (top, left).

DER ROSENKAVALIER

Richard Strauss felt that, for his own music, the past was as important as the future. *Der Rosenkavalier*, or *The Rose Bearer*, is a romantic comedy set in the aristocratic world of 18th-century Vienna. First performed in Dresden in 1911, it was a huge and instant success. The music uses Viennese waltzes to create a world of humor, intrigue, and nostalgia — just as if the violent upheavals of *Salome* and *Elektra* had never happened.

Strauss (seated, center) *and his colleagues*

FINDING LIFE IN THE OLD WAYS

Hans Pfitzner (1869–1949) and Erich Wolfgang Korngold (1897–1957) were both conservative composers. Pfitzner created a masterpiece with his opera *Palestrina*, about a 16th-century Italian composer staying true to his genius despite political and religious pressures. Korngold, a child prodigy, was only thirteen when he wrote his first ballet, *Der Schneemann*, or *The Snowman*. Although a traditional composer, Alexander von Zemlinsky (1871–1942) was also interested in the modernist world of Gustav Mahler.

Richard Strauss's opera Salome, *based on writer Oscar Wilde's play, was considered so shocking it was banned in several cities.*

Ferruccio Busoni (1866–1924) was a gifted Italian composer and pianist.

BREAKING WITH THE PAST

German composer Richard Wagner (1813–1883) lit a slow-burning fuse with the intensity and complex chromatic harmonies of his operas, which were, and still are, fiercely controversial works. Fifty years later, the musical explosion occurred in the work of Austrian Arnold Schoenberg (1874–1951) and his two most gifted pupils. *Atonal*, which means "not in any musical key," describes Schoenberg's music from 1908 onward.

RELUCTANT REVOLUTIONARY

Arnold Schoenberg was a gifted teacher of composition who thoroughly grounded his pupils in the musical styles of the past. His own music, however, was so radical that it left tradition far behind. At the 1908 premiere of his Second String Quartet, in Vienna, many people were appalled by the work's rootless, floating harmony. Others sensed the discovery of a thrilling new world of music.

In the early 20th century, Vienna was the capital city of the Austro-Hungarian Empire. Its great tradition of classical music continues to this day.

Berg (left) *and Webern* (right) *were Schoenberg's two most talented students. Although very different characters with very different musical styles, they remained lifelong friends.*

Vienna's exciting and thriving musical life was built on the city's solid foundation of commercial strength.

HIS MASTER'S VOICE — UP TO A POINT

Austrian Anton von Webern (1883–1945) was a student and great admirer of Arnold Schoenberg. As a young composer, Webern followed his teacher's example but developed it further in his own musical direction. Webern's music from this period is extremely spare and concentrated. For example, his Five Pieces for Orchestra, written between 1911 and 1913, lasts less than five minutes all together.

DIFFERENT FROM THE START

Alban Berg (1885–1935), another of Schoenberg's students, tried, briefly, to work in Webern's ultra-compressed style. Schoenberg advised him, however, to go back to tackling larger forms. The outcome was Berg's early masterpiece, the violent and darkly colored Three Orchestral Pieces, written between 1914 and 1915.

PIERROT LUNAIRE

A cycle of twenty-one poems written, originally, in French, *Pierrot Lunaire* explores the disturbed mind of a moonstruck Italian clown. Schoenberg used a German translation to set the poems for an actress or a singer and five instruments. In doing so, he invented *Sprechstimme*, or "spoken musical voice," a technical device that seeks the boundary between singing and normal speech.

Master composer Arnold Schoenberg

The Viennese have always been passionate about opera.

9

IMPRESSIONISM AND SYMBOLISM

IParis, at the turn of the century, was Europe's most colorful center of artistic life. As painters, composers, and writers were shaking off the academic restrictions of the past, the atmosphere of this free-spirited city attracted talent from other countries, most notably, Sergei Diaghilev's Ballets Russes.

In the early 1900s, the exotic costume designs for the Ballets Russes were all the rage.

Claude Debussy was very fond of his daughter Claude-Emma, nicknamed Chouchou. In 1908, he completed Children's Corner, *six piano pieces dedicated to Chouchou, who died in 1919 at the age of fourteen.*

Debussy (right) believed passionately that music needed to be freed from the stale, predictable "chains" of academic tradition. Although Erik Satie (left) agreed with Debussy, Satie's simple but subtle compositions puzzled many concert-goers, who expected something far more spectacular.

A POET OF MYSTERY

The music of French composer Claude Debussy (1862–1918) launched a quiet but bold revolution. "In the opera house, they sing too much," he said. So his only completed opera, *Pelléas et Mélisande* (1893–1902), introduced a new style of composition for the stage — vivid, atmospheric, and understated. In orchestral masterworks, such as *La Mer* (1905) and *Images* (1912), and in his piano music, Debussy further explored his flair for supple rhythms and shades of instrumental coloring.

A MASTER OF THE ORCHESTRA

Frenchman Maurice Ravel (1875–1937) liked to evoke exotic sounds and ancient worlds within more sharply defined structures than Debussy. His piano works, especially, are more brilliant than Debussy's. Ravel's masterpiece, the ballet *Daphnis et Chloé*, set in ancient Greece, was first performed by the Ballets Russes in 1912.

ARTISTIC INSPIRATION

Composers from all over Europe were drawn to Paris by the city's cosmopolitan appeal. Two Spaniards, Isaac Albéniz (1860–1909) and Manuel de Falla (1876–1946), wrote some of their finest works there. Albéniz's *Ibéria* is one of the masterpieces of Spanish piano music. French composers Gabriel Fauré (1845–1924) and Erik Satie (1866–1925) also composed some of their best work in the energizing Parisian atmosphere. Some reviewers criticized Satie's piano pieces, describing them as "shapeless." Satie responded by composing more.

Gabriel Fauré was greatly respected by younger composers. Here, he plays the piano at his home in Paris, with his friend Isaac Albéniz (left, with cigar) looking on.

ART IN PARIS

Paris was a focal point of development in all the arts. The Impressionist paintings of Claude Monet (1840–1926) have often been described as the visual counterpart to Claude Debussy's muted, half-toned music. Debussy, however, preferred the work of other, different painters, such as American James Whistler (1834–1903), who Debussy once described as "the greatest creator of mysterious effects in art."

Whistler's Nocturne: Blue and Silver - Chelsea

FOLK SONG IN EUROPE

Much of central Europe, including what are now Hungary, Slovakia, and the Czech Republic, was, at the start of the 20th century, part of the Austro-Hungarian Empire ruled by the Hapsburg dynasty of Franz Joseph I in Vienna. Political nationalism, however, had been growing throughout the Empire for decades. Composers began to reflect this nationalism in their music.

When he was eleven years old, Leos Janácek was sent to this monastery (in the background, with spire) in Brno, Moravia, to sing as a choirboy.

THE PEOPLE SING AND DANCE

The early works of Hungarian composer Béla Bartók (1881–1945) were influenced by the German concert-hall tradition of Richard Strauss. Bartók's discovery of Hungarian and Transylvanian folk music brought about a radical change when he blended these two different musical worlds into his own style of dissonant harmony and driving dance rhythms. A brilliant composer-pianist, Bartók also wrote for the stage, with his opera, *Bluebeard's Castle* (1911), and two ballets, *The Wooden Prince* (1914–1916) and *The Miraculous Mandarin* (1918–1919).

Although Bartók (seated, left) *was an instinctive modernist and Kodály* (far right) *a more tuneful traditionalist, both were musically committed to the cause of the Hungarian people.*

12

THE COMPOSER AS TEACHER

Zoltán Kodály (1882–1967) traveled and worked together with Béla Bartók to collect and record Hungarian and Transylvanian folk music. The experience influenced Kodály's own relaxed and pictorial musical style. A gifted teacher, Kodály started a tradition of choral singing in Hungarian schools that still thrives today.

FROM SPEECH TO SONG

Born in the Czech region of Moravia, Leos Janácek (1854–1928) was another folk music collector. He sketched, in musical terms, the everyday phrases he heard spoken around him in the city streets of Brno and the Moravian countryside, saying "I am trying to get close to the heart of humble Czech people." The result was a concise, vivid style of vocal writing.

Bartók (fourth from the left) traveled throughout Hungary, asking people to record their folk songs on his Edison's Phonograph. These recordings deeply influenced his music.

Budapest was Hungary's capital city, but political and cultural control remained mostly with Germans appointed by the Hapsburg Empire. Kodály and Bartók were among the artists who wanted this German control to change.

ROMANY MUSICIANS

Although the population had started to move toward the cities, central Europe in the early 20th century was still a largely rural world of small towns and poor villages. The folk music tradition of the countryside was dying out, but Bartók and Kodály found it still surviving, kept alive especially by the Romany people.

The traveling Romany people were the folk musicians of eastern Europe.

13

REVERIE AND REVOLUTION

Reverie imperial Russia under the rule of Tsar Nicholas II was provincial and authoritarian. Ignoring the outcries of the Russian people, the government found it increasingly difficult to suppress popular demands for political change. In much the same way, Russian composers found themselves divided — into those who approved of and accepted their world as it was, and those who saw themselves as angry radicals.

THE YOUNG REBEL

Russian pianist Sergei Prokofiev (1891–1953) upset his teachers at St. Petersburg Conservatory with his aggressively rhythmic works and the extravagant style of his Second Piano Concerto (1913). After composing his wry and engaging first symphony, the "Classical," in 1918, Prokofiev decided to leave post-Revolutionary Russia for a new life in the United States.

REVOLUTION IN RUSSIA

In 1905, the "revolution" in Russia was actually a surge of unrest following the shooting of unarmed civilian protesters. Widespread famine and the misery of World War I finally triggered the overthrow of Tsar Nicholas II in February 1917. The following October, Vladimir Lenin's Bolshevik Party seized power, after which decades of Communist rule suppressed the creativity and independent thought of almost all composers.

Alexander Scriabin was also a remarkable pianist. As a child, he practiced so hard the piano pedal wore through the sole of his shoe.

Sergei Prokofiev was a brilliant pianist. While still a student, he composed works that extended the boundaries of piano technique.

Revolution brews in Imperial Russia.

Sergei Rachmaninov was the music director of the Bolshoi Opera from 1904 to 1906. Shown behind him are two singers from his opera Francesca da Rimini (1906).

A LATE, GREAT ROMANTIC

The success of his Second Piano Concerto, in 1901, launched Sergei Rachmaninov (1873–1943) into a triple career as composer, conductor, and one of the century's great pianists. His passionate, melancholic music remained true to the tradition and spirit of Russian Romanticism. Rachmaninov did not feel there was a place for him in post-Revolutionary Russia. In 1918, he and his family traveled to Scandinavia and New York and eventually settled in the United States.

Costumes for a ballet based on Scheherazade, by Nikolai Rimsky-Korsakov (1844–1908), were designed by Léon Bakst (1866–1924), a Russian artist who gained international fame for his work with the Ballets Russes.

15

A MESSIANIC COMPOSER

Prerevolutionary Russia was home to many strange, semireligious cults. Russian composer-pianist Alexander Scriabin (1872–1915) saw himself as a Messiah figure for future music. Scriabin wanted to build a temple in India in which to perform his Final Mystery for piano, massed choirs, orchestra, and an imaginary form of light-projection. Only sketches for the project survive. The shimmering orchestration of Scriabin's Poem of Ecstasy (1908) gives audiences an idea of what Final Mystery may have sounded like.

PUCCINI AND OPERA

In Italy, opera was an exciting and beloved musical art form. When the great Giuseppe Verdi (1813–1901) died, his status as the uncrowned king of Italian opera passed to Giacomo Puccini (1858–1924). Meanwhile, other composers were trying to steer Italian music toward a new future.

Puccini's heroine

TRYING TO STAY ON TOP

Pietro Mascagni (1863–1945) claimed to have single-handedly launched the *verismo*, or "reality," movement in opera with *Cavalleria Rusticana* (1889), a one-act opera about Sicilian peasant life. Worldwide fame, however, did not help him achieve another huge success, even though *Isabeau* (1911) and *Lodoletta* (1917) are sometimes performed today. Although Mascagni and Puccini once shared lodgings, Mascagni later became jealous of his star rival. Ruggiero Leoncavallo (1857–1919) also was unable to repeat the success of *Pagliacci* (1892). His comedy *Zazà* (1900), however, came close.

Mascagni (left) and Puccini (right) flank composer Alberto Franchetti (1806–1942) at the piano. Puccini's career began less successfully than Mascagni's, but Puccini turned his early mistakes into lasting triumphs.

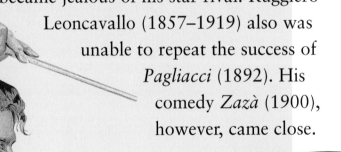

Cavalleria Rusticana, *or* Rustic Chivalry, *made Mascagni famous overnight.*

16

MADAM BUTTERFLY

In February 1904, the audience at Milan's La Scala opera house watched Puccini's *Madam Butterfly* in silence. Newspaper headlines the next day called *Madam Butterfly* a "flop." Puccini immediately revised the opera about a Japanese girl who is abandoned by her husband, an American naval officer, and kills herself in despair. The version that premiered three months later has long since been one of Puccini's greatest hits.

Puccini's Tosca *is set in 19th-century Rome. The heroine, Floria Tosca, watches her lover Cavaradossi, a political prisoner, go through what they both believe is a mock execution by a firing squad. The bullets, however, are real.*

In 1910, Puccini completed La Fanciulla del West, *or* The Girl of the Golden West, *for New York's Metropolitan Opera House.*

SHOCK, HORROR — THE PUBLIC LOVED IT

The late 19th century had seen the rise of *verismo* in opera. Its followers insisted that traditional grand opera had had its day, and down-to-earth, tragic stories now deserved a place on the operatic stage. Giacomo Puccini took hold of that idea in his wildly successful *Tosca* (1900), in which the heroine murders the villain after listening to the screams of her lover being tortured offstage.

BACK TO THE FUTURE

Gian Francesco Malipiero (1882–1973) greatly admired his country's rich musical heritage, especially the works of Claudio Monteverdi (1567–1643). This music inspired Malipiero to blend, in his own compositions, its sharply focused style of expression with modern European developments. Alfredo Casella (1883–1947) also looked beyond his Italian background. His work was influenced by Richard Strauss and Gustav Mahler and, later, by Igor Stravinsky and Béla Bartók.

17

NORDIC SYMPHONIES

Musical life in northern European countries had always trailed behind the great powerhouses of Italy, Germany, Austria, and France. Finland did not even have a symphony orchestra until 1884, yet this remote country produced Jean Sibelius, one of the century's greatest composers. Nearby Denmark gave the world Carl Nielsen.

Carl Nielsen came from the Danish island of Odense. His father taught him to play the violin and the piano.

A MIGHTY VOICE FROM THE NORTH

As a student in Helsinki, Finland, Jean Sibelius (1865–1957) dreamed of becoming a violin virtuoso. When this plan didn't work out, he studied composition in Berlin and Vienna. Returning to Finland, which was then part of the Russian empire, Sibelius became involved in the Finnish nationalist movement for independence. Finnish folk stories and poetry inspired his early works. The success of those works soon made Sibelius a national hero. The tune of his

Composer-pianist Ferruccio Busoni (left) and Jean Sibelius (right) were old friends. In his memoirs, British conductor Sir Henry Wood recalled, "I never knew where they would get to . . . They were like a couple of irresponsible schoolboys."

symphonic poem *Finlandia* (1900) became Finland's unofficial national anthem. Sibelius found fame abroad, especially in Britain and America, with his cycle of seven symphonies.

PROGRESSIVE TONALITY

Danish composer Carl Nielsen (1865–1931) first earned his living as a violinist and played in the 1892 premiere of his First Symphony. Over the next decade, Nielsen became an important composer and teacher, also composing operas for Copenhagen's Royal Danish Theatre. His comic opera *Maskarade* (1906) is regarded as Denmark's national masterpiece. Nielsen developed the unusual technique of "progressive tonality," by which a symphony travels toward an ending that is in a different musical key than the one in which it began. His Fourth Symphony (1916), subtitled "The Inextinguishable," reflects his ideas about the relationship of music to life. "Music is life," Nielsen once said. "Like life, it cannot be extinguished."

Nielsen's music quickly became known outside of Denmark. This program of orchestral works was handed out at the famous concert hall, Concertgebouw, in Amsterdam in 1912.

Sibelius was a darkly brooding man who did not like to be photographed.

19

"Land of a Thousand Lakes"

MUSIC AND NATURE

For Sibelius, music and the Finnish landscape went together. He built large musical structures out of repeated, endlessly developed fragments of melody — an idea that came partly from his research into Finnish folk singing. The result was a spare, but powerful and highly effective, way of composing that often suggested the vast, empty spaces of the snowbound Finnish countryside.

BLUES, JAZZ, AND RAGTIME

Blues was the original music of America's black population. It emerged from the cotton plantations of the deep South and made its way north to the big cities. Jazz made a similar journey, spreading out from its roots in New Orleans to conquer the world. Both had an influence on classical music, in America and beyond.

I GOT THE BLUES

Blues allowed musicians to improvise against the fixed shapes and rhythms of verses. It flourished in vaudeville, the South's style of music-hall entertainment, and produced such great singers as "Ma" Rainey (1886–1939), Bessie Smith (1894–1937), and Clara Smith (1895–1935).

Her powerful delivery and brilliant way of timing a phrase led Bessie Smith to become one of the biggest blues stars in history. Once a member of "Ma" Rainey's vaudeville troupe, she died tragically in an automobile accident at age forty-three.

Scott Joplin once heard a recording of the overture to Wagner's opera Tannhäuser, *but he was barred from hearing enough classical music to develop his own composing technique.*

SYNCOPATED RHYTHMS

Ragtime was usually piano music, with the right hand playing in "ragged time" against the left hand's regular, rhythmic patterns — a technique known as syncopation. Scott Joplin (1868–1917), the century's foremost ragtime pianist, was the gifted composer of the "Maple Leaf Rag" and "The Entertainer". Joplin also wrote two operas, *A Guest of Honor* (1903) and *Treemonisha* (1911), but his operatic ambitions were thwarted by discrimination. At that time, black people were not allowed in opera houses.

Born Gertrude Pridgett, in Columbus, Georgia, "Ma" Rainey took her name from her vaudeville-dancer husband, William "Pa" Rainey. She was known as "Mother of the Blues."

JAZZ SWEEPS AMERICA

The roots of jazz overlapped those of blues and ragtime, and it was played as much as it was sung. Jazz bands had the trumpet, trombone, and clarinet as improvising soloists with a rhythm section of guitar or banjo, drums, string bass, and piano.

THE GREAT AMERICAN MUSICAL

From operettas and variety shows came the "musical," a combination of story, song, and dance. On Broadway, in New York City, George M. Cohan (1878–1942) wrote and directed a string of hits, including *Little Johnny Jones* (1904) and *The Honeymooners* (1907). Victor Herbert (1859–1924) wrote songs for *Babes in Toyland* (1903) and other shows. Irving Berlin (1888–1989) gained fame with his song "Alexander's Ragtime Band" (1911) and the shows *Watch Your Step* (1914) and *Stop! Look! Listen!* (1915).

Blues originated in the cotton fields of the South, but jazz has always been city music. Its home is the colorful city of New Orleans, Louisiana, on the Mississippi River Delta.

21

TUXEDO BAND

When the original Tuxedo Band made its early jazz recordings in 1917, the music had already traveled a long way from its origins among black Americans in the South. The band played in New York City and produced several musicians, including Clarence Williams, who later became jazz stars in their own right. Jazz had become the favorite entertainment of rich, white and poor, black audiences alike.

The Tuxedo Band with Clarence Williams (bottom, center)

FROM ROMANTICISM TO IVES

Classical music in early 20th-century America was an imported, 19th-century European product directed toward prosperous, middle-class communities in towns and cities. Against this elite, conventional background, the wild originality of Charles Ives (1874–1954) came like a bolt from the blue.

George W. Chadwick studied in Germany, then returned to teach music at Boston's New England Conservatory.

EUROPEAN INHERITANCE

American Edward MacDowell (1860–1908) studied piano and techniques of composition in France and Germany. When he returned home, he played, composed, and taught at Columbia University, and he relaxed by conducting a men's glee club. MacDowell's music does not sound particularly American. He was a genuinely Romantic spirit. Americans George Chadwick (1854–1931) and Arthur Foote (1853–1937) also composed successfully within the musical forms of Europe's classical tradition.

Arthur Foote studied at Harvard University with American composer John Knowles Paine (1839–1906), then settled in Boston, where he became an admired composer, organist, and teacher.

A COMPOSER BEFORE HER TIME

When musical prodigy Amy Beach (1867–1944) married at age eighteen, her husband asked her to cut back on her appearances as a concert pianist. He said composing was a more suitable occupation for a married woman. She produced over three hundred works under the name of Mrs. H. H. A. Beach.

AMY BEACH

"No other life than that of a musician could ever have been possible for me," wrote Amy Beach. Even so, it took all her determination to succeed in a man's world. Only after her husband died in 1910 was she able to start touring Europe as a concert pianist. Her strongest music has real passion, yet still reflects a European influence.

Amy Beach was a true pioneer among American composers.

The music of Charles Ives explored advanced ideas, such as "polytonality," which involves different sections of an orchestra playing in different keys at the same time. In Central Park in the Dark (1906), orchestral sounds suggesting the quietness of the empty park are increasingly overlaid by noisy bursts of jazzlike music from a nearby café. These sounds are played at the same time by different orchestras in different tempos, thereby requiring two conductors. Nothing quite like it had ever been composed before.

A NEW ENGLAND MAVERICK

Charles Ives was American classical music's first genius. The son of a bandmaster in Danbury, Connecticut, Ives absorbed all the different sounds of the world around him — hymns, popular songs, and bands, in addition to classical music. Ignoring every conventional rule, he assembled his musical ideas into tapestries of sound that were daring and dissonant. For instance, in "Puttnam's Camp" from *Three Places in New England* (1908–1914), the orchestra imitates several bands playing at once. Because Ives was also in the insurance business, he could compose only on weekends. His music sounded very modern for its time and only began to be appreciated near the end of his life. Many of his works were not heard until years after they were written.

Ives tried to capture the bustling activity of the city in his music.

STRAVINSKY

Igor Stravinsky leaped to fame as a composer after a questionable and unpromising beginning. In 1909, he was an unknown former pupil of traditional Russian composer Nikolai Rimsky-Korsakov, who, at first, did not think Stravinsky had much talent. Just four years later, however, Stravinsky had written three fantastic ballet scores. Each of them unleashed a rhythmic firepower that changed western music forever.

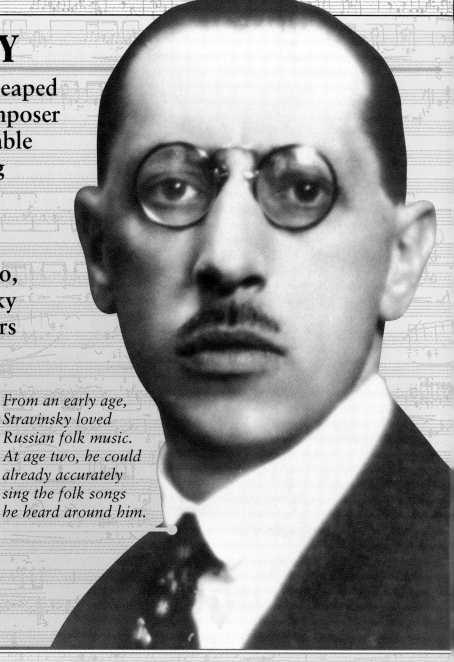

From an early age, Stravinsky loved Russian folk music. At age two, he could already accurately sing the folk songs he heard around him.

HOW TO MEET A DEADLINE

Stravinsky owed his breakthrough to Sergei Diaghilev (1872–1929), the Russian impresario who founded the Ballets Russes dance company. In 1909, a commission for the company's Paris season needed a composer on short notice. Diaghilev took a chance on Stravinsky, who worked at lightning speed and completed *The Firebird*, based on a Russian folktale, in just five months. *The Firebird* was a sensation. Stravinsky became famous overnight and worked with the Ballets Russes for many years.

The ungainly appearance of Nijinsky's dancers was shocking.

Stravinsky (seated, second from right) is joined by colleagues from the Ballets Russes, including costume designer Léon Bakst (standing, far right).

Stravinsky's second ballet, Petrushka, *came one year after* The Firebird.

A PUPPET DANCES

Diaghilev wanted more "hits," and Stravinsky provided them. In 1911, he composed the ballet *Petrushka.* Its daring use of bi-tonality, presenting musical ideas in two different keys at the same time, broke new ground. The story is about the sad love life of a puppet with many human qualities in a fairground show in the city of St. Petersburg in Russia. To portray this world, Stravinsky uses disconnected blocks of orchestral sound held together by the rhythmic energy that drives them along. The idea was new. Stravinsky took it even further.

THE RIOT OF SPRING

The first performance of *The Rite of Spring,* in 1913, started the most famous riot in musical history. By the standards of classical ballet, the story was X-rated — at an imaginary ceremony, a young girl dances herself to death. The music's pounding rhythms and extreme dissonance outraged the audience. After a triumphant performance the following year, however, Stravinsky was carried shoulder-high through the streets of Paris by a crowd of admirers.

AHEAD OF HIS TIME

The audience's fury at the premiere of *The Rite of Spring* was probably more of a reaction to Nijinsky's choreography than to Stravinsky's music. Classical ballet emphasizes gravity-defying lightness, and the dancers' feet point outward. In his attempt to convey the music's earth-stamping power in visual terms, Nijinsky had his dancers do the opposite. In the process, this dancer-choreographer had begun to invent modern dance.

Vaslav Nijinsky (1890–1950) was the most gifted dancer of his time and the biggest draw of the Ballets Russes. His virtuoso performance in the title role of Petrushka *was the talk of Paris in the summer of 1911. Nijinsky also had bold, experimental ambitions as a choreographer.*

SUNSET AND DAWN

SIn the early 20th century, the British Empire was so large it was described as a realm where "the Sun never sets." England's composers, however, preferred to stand aside from this apparently secure and serene world, which was soon to be engulfed in a mechanized war. Some reacted against it and turned instead, for ideas and inspiration, to their country's musical grass roots.

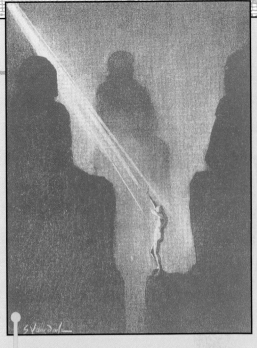

Edward Elgar's oratorio is now one of his most beloved works. At its first performance, however, the choir and musicians found the music strange and difficult. This illustration portrays the journey of Gerontius's soul, after death, toward the sight of God.

MARCHING TO A DARKER DREAM

The pride of the British Empire seemed to speak through the popular and patriotic music of composer Edward Elgar (1857–1934), such as his *Pomp and Circumstance Marches*. The tune "Land of Hope and Glory" comes from one of these marches. The real Elgar, however, appears in much larger and deeper works, such as his oratorio, *The Dream of Gerontius* (1900), and his two symphonies. These works contain dark warnings of upheavals to come and reflect the inner strength Elgar drew from his Catholic faith.

Elgar was interested in gramophone recordings, and he made some of the earliest ones. In this photo, the device in front of Elgar funneled the sound of the orchestra toward a microphone.

GO WEST, YOUNG MAN

Englishman Frederick Delius (1862–1934) was sent by his father to Florida to manage an orange grove. Delius's music was marked for life by the tropical glow of his surroundings and the sound of black male voices singing as they worked. On returning to Europe, where he lived mostly in France, he produced two radiant masterworks, his opera, *A Village Romeo and Juliet* (1901), a tragic story of young love that is set in Switzerland, and his antireligious oratorio, *A Mass of Life* (1905).

Delius had strong links with the German and Scandinavian cultures. The mountain landscapes of Norway inspired A Song of the High Hills *(1911) for wordless chorus and orchestra.*

THE COUNTRYSIDE ENDURES

Wanting to renew the deepest values of traditional English music, Ralph Vaughan Williams (1872–1958) went "back to basics" in a different way. He edited the tunes of English hymns, researched English music of earlier centuries, and collected folk songs from the English countryside. Williams combined all these influences in works such as *Fantasia on a Theme of Thomas Tallis* (1910) and *The Lark Ascending* (1914). *A Sea Symphony* (1909) is a choral setting for words by acclaimed American poet Walt Whitman.

THE PLANETS

Gustav Holst (1874–1934) and Ralph Vaughan Williams shared a common interest in folk music, and they collected it together. Holst also had more exotic interests, such as the astrological signs that inspired his orchestral suite *The Planets* (1914–1917). Many believed that the battering rhythms of this work's opening movement, "Mars, the Bringer of War," were a vision of World War I, but Holst always denied this.

A postage stamp commemorates Holst's most famous work.

Holst composed for choirs and opera, as well as for orchestras. Savitri *(1908) is a chamber opera based on a Hindu story. The* Hymn of Jesus *(1917) is for chorus and orchestra.*

WAR DESTROYS THE OLD WORLD

World War I began in August 1914. When it ended, more than four years later, Europe was a different place. The defeated German and Austro-Hungarian empires were divided by the exhausted victors Britain and France, while Russia descended into the dark chaos of revolution. The lives of composers, like the lives of everyone else, changed.

STARTING AGAIN

During the war, Igor Stravinsky lived in the neutral country of Switzerland. Conditions during wartime made the lavish productions of the Ballets Russes no longer possible. So Stravinsky decided to move in a new direction, writing works for much smaller forces. He arranged Russian folk songs and sketched out a Russian ballet, *Les Noces*, or *The Wedding*, (1914–1917). *Renard*, or *The Fox*, (1916) was a bolder idea. It was a story about farmyard animals that were portrayed by singers and acrobats.

28

Arnold Schoenberg spent the war in and out of the Austrian army. Webern, his former student, constantly petitioned authorities to exempt Schoenberg from military duty because of his national importance as a composer.

THE SOLDIER'S TALE

Working with Swiss poet C. F. Ramuz, Stravinsky composed *The Soldier's Tale* (1918) for a traveling theater group. This story, about a soldier who sells his soul to the devil in exchange for love and riches, is portrayed by actors, a dancer, and a group of seven musicians. Stravinsky had created the first example of musical theater.

Stravinsky (seated) *and Debussy*

Photographs like this one, which was probably posed, suggested that the front line was not such a bad place to be in World War I. In reality, however, the mechanized slaughter, poison gas, and mud were a nightmare from which Europe perhaps has never completely recovered.

STAIRWAY TO HEAVEN

Like his pupils Anton von Webern and Alban Berg, Arnold Schoenberg was drafted into the Austrian army. During his on-and-off wartime service, he composed *Die Jakobsleiter*, or *Jacob's Ladder*, (1917) which was planned as a vast oratorio about the meeting of Heaven and Earth that the biblical figure of Jacob saw in a dream. Schoenberg never completed it, but the unfinished oratorio is, nevertheless, one of his greatest achievements.

DIFFERENT RESPONSES

When the war broke out, Maurice Ravel quickly completed one of his finest works, Piano Trio (1914). He then joined the military, driving an ambulance at the Western Front. Growing increasingly ill with cancer, Claude Debussy wrote a brilliant set of piano études in 1915. Richard Strauss continued his composing almost as if the war did not exist. In 1919, he completed his grandest opera, *Die Frau ohne Schatten*, or *The Woman without a Shadow*.

Richard Strauss kept composing throughout the war years. Besides his work on the score of Die Frau ohne Schatten, *he wrote a chamber opera,* Ariadne auf Naxos *(1916).*

Although it meant he had to stop composing for a while, Ravel felt it was his duty to serve France during the war.

· TIME LINE ·

	WORLD EVENTS	MUSICAL EVENTS	THE ARTS	FAMOUS MUSICIANS	MUSICAL WORKS
1900	•China: Boxer Rebellion	•Leoncavallo: Zazà •Puccini: Tosca	•Death of Oscar Wilde	•Aaron Copland born	•Mahler: Fourth Symphony
1901	•First transatlantic radio transmission	•Rachmaninov: Second Piano Concerto	•Thomas Mann: Buddenbrooks	•Jascha Heifetz born	•Elgar: Pomp and Circumstance March no. 1
1902	•South Africa: second Boer War ends	•Enrico Caruso: first recordings	•Joseph Conrad: Heart of Darkness	•Omer Simeon born	•Debussy: Pelléas et Mélisande
1903	•Wright brothers complete first powered flight	•Janáček: Jenufa	•Jack London: Call of the Wild	•Ben Pollack born	•Schoenberg: Pelleas und Melisande
1904	•Japan and Russia at war (to 1905)	•Puccini's Madam Butterfly flops in Milan	•Chekhov's The Cherry Orchard is first staged	•Coleman Hawkins born	•Debussy: L'Isle Joyeuse
1905	•Russia: first revolution	•Lehár: The Merry Widow	•Paris: first Fauve exhibition	•Cecil Scott born	•Richard Strauss: Salome
1906	•U.S.: San Francisco earthquake	• Nielsen: Maskarade	•Death of Henrik Ibsen	•Dmitri Shostakovich born	•Schoenberg: First Chamber Symphony
1907	•Maiden voyage of the ocean liner Lusitania	•Janáček: Osud	•Picasso: first cubist art Les Demoiselles d'Avignon	•Death of Edvard Grieg	•Sibelius: Third Symphony
1908	•Henry Ford launches Model T car	•Schoenberg: first atonal works	•Brancusi: early versions of The Kiss	•Olivier Messiaen born	•Mahler: Das Lied von der Erde
1909	•Blériot flies across the English Channel	•Paris: first appearance of the Ballets Russes	•Italy's Futurist movement publishes its manifesto	•Gil Rodin born	•Webern: Six Orchestral Pieces, op. 6
1910	•Japan takes control of Korea	•Stravinsky: The Firebird	•Kandinsky: Cossacks	•Art Tatum born	•Alban Berg: String Quartet, op. 3
1911	•Chinese revolution: emperor overthrown	•Strauss: Der Rosenkavalier	•Matisse: Still Life with Goldfish	•Death of Gustav Mahler	•Irving Berlin: "Alexander's Ragtime Band"
1912	•Balkan Wars (to 1913) •Titanic sinks	•Ravel: Daphnis et Chloé	•Death of August Strindberg	•John Cage born	•Schoenberg: Pierrot Lunaire
1913	•Henry Ford invents the assembly line	•Riot at Stravinsky's The Rite of Spring	•First International Exhibition of Modern Art	•Benjamin Britten born	•Debussy: Jeux
1914	•World War I begins	•Irving Berlin: Watch Your Step	•Edgar Rice Burroughs: Tarzan of the Apes	•Billie Holiday born	•Vaughan Williams: The Lark Ascending
1915	•ANZAC troops slaughtered on Gallipoli	•Irving Berlin: Stop! Look! Listen!	•D. H. Lawrence: The Rainbow	•Frank Sinatra born	•Debussy: Études
1916	•Ireland: Easter Rising in Dublin	•Strauss: Ariadne auf Naxos	•Monet: Water Lilies series	•Yehudi Menuhin born	•Nielsen: Fourth Symphony
1917	•Russian Revolution •U.S. enters World War I	•Original Dixieland Jazz Band: first recordings	•Dutch avant-garde artists publish magazine De Stijl		•George M. Cohan: "Over There"
1918	•World War I ends •UK: women get vote	•Louis Armstrong plays with King Oliver's band	•Lytton Strachey: Eminent Victorians	•Leonard Bernstein born	•Stravinsky: The Soldier's Tale
1919	•Treaty of Versailles •Nazi Party founded		•Bauhaus design school founded in Germany	•Margot Fonteyn born	•Strauss: Die Frau ohne Schatten

GLOSSARY

chromatic: describing music that uses all twelve notes of the chromatic scale to form differing and sometimes extreme harmonies.

concerto: a piece of music with three contrasting movements that is written for solo instruments and an orchestra.

dissonance: a mixing or clashing of two or more musical notes that, when played together, produce a harsh, unstable sound.

études: musical "studies," or pieces of music composed more for the practice of technique than for their artistic value.

glee club: an amateur chorus that usually sings short pieces, often without being accompanied by instruments.

impresario: a person who manages, promotes, or conducts a concert company.

opera: a musical drama that includes vocal pieces accompanied by an orchestra, as well as orchestral overtures and interludes.

oratorio: a long choral work, usually on a religious subject, that includes recitations, solo voices, and choruses, without action or scenery.

provincial: narrow-minded; characterized by a limited interest or outlook.

symphonic poem: an orchestral work that tells a story or depicts a scene, usually in a single movement and with a freer form than a symphony

symphony: a long and usually complex musical composition for an orchestra, traditionally composed with four movements, but could have several more movements or only one movement, and may include solo or choral voices.

virtuoso: a highly skilled musical performer.

MORE BOOKS TO READ

Billie Holiday: The Tragedy and Triumph of Lady Day. Leslie Gourse (Franklin Watts)

Classical Music: The 50 Greatest Composers and Their 1,000 Greatest Works. Phil G. Goulding (Ballantine Books)

The Great Composers: An Illustrated Guide to the Lives, Key Works, and Influences of Over 120 Renowned Composers. Wendy Thompson (Lorenz Books)

Introducing Stravinsky. Introducing Composers (series). Roland Vernon (Chelsea House)

Jazz: An American Saga. James Lincoln Collier (Henry Holt & Co.)

The Story of the Orchestra. Robert Levine (Black Dog & Leventhal)

The Young Person's Guide to the Opera. Anita Ganeri and Nicola Barber (Harcourt Brace)

WEB SITES

Classical Music Pages: Giacomo Puccini (1858–1924). *w3.rz-berlin.mpg.de/cmp/puccini.html*

Claude Debussy and Impressionism. *www.classicalmus.hispeed.com/articles/debussy.html*

Early 20th Century (1900–1930). *www.hearts-ease.org/ cgi-bin/index_c.cgi?period=Early%2020th%20Century*

I Hear America Singing: Profiles. *www.pbs.org/wnet/ihas/profiles.html*

Les Ballets Russes de Diaghilev 1909–1929. *www.dmu.ac.uk/~jafowler/russes.html*

Ma Rainey. *www.blueflamecafe.com/Ma_Rainey.html*

Due to the dynamic nature of the Internet, some web sites stay current longer than others. To find additional web sites, use a reliable search engine with one or more of the following keywords: *Bartók, Amy Beach, Irving Berlin, gramophone, jazz, Scott Joplin,* Madam Butterfly, *Mahler,* Arnold Schoenberg, Bessie Smith, and *Igor Stravinsky.*

INDEX

32